Hey, Sis!

Notes of Encouragement for Faith-Filled Sister-Friends

Kimberly DeAnn

NEWMAN SPRINGS PUBLISHING
320 Broad Street
Red Bank, NJ 07701

First originally published by Newman Springs Publishing 2024

ISBN 979-8-88763-303-9 (Paperback)
ISBN 979-8-88763-871-3 (Hardcover)
ISBN 979-8-88763-304-6 (Digital)

Printed in the United States of America

In honor of the women who came before me, grateful for those who have walked alongside me and with ardency for my daughter, bonus daughters and grand-daughters, I write these words: Fully accepted, fiercely loved, and already more than enough is the freedom we should be walking in, the position we should be loving from, and the faith we can hold *God-fidently* to!

With so much love,
Kim

Introduction

Of all the hurts, hang-ups, and habits that hinder us, those strongholds that hold us back from all we were meant to be and that which we are called to do, I believe that what cripples us most is faulty thinking! Yep, stinking thinking!

I know because the mental gymnastics of "Do good, be good" haunted me my entire life. Most often, the mountain that needed moving was *me*! My own thinking patterns had caused a level of cognitive dissonance that was sure to do me in. Something had to change!

Seven years of taking authority over my thought life culminated into a deep desire to help other passionate but weary God gals to do the same. I found a better way, and I want you to, as well! With every pen stroke, because it didn't start out digital, I pray you feel the love of a sister who's rooting for you, cheering you on, and speaking truth and love into your very heart…one encouraging love note at a time!

Ardently,
Kim

Hey Sis,

Yes, you, that energetic and eager one, the gal wrapping up her twenties and looking forward to being *thirty something* because then, maybe they'll take you seriously at work. Maybe your mother will stop overparenting and trying to micromanage your life. You'll be legit and respected. That whole decade of trying to figure out who you are will be behind you. You'll be experienced and finally, it will be your time to shine! Yep, I'm talking to you, Ma'am…I admire that zeal and independence in you. But, please know you're gonna need Jesus heading into your thirties.

And you, my even wiser, more disciplined late thirties momma. Whew, I know you're tired, but you aren't finished yet. You've still got it, so don't you dare start feeling like some kind of low-hanging fruit. Those thirties were a little harder than you thought they'd be, but you are better for all the sacrifices and hard choices you made. I bet you're thanking God for Mom now. What would you have done without her? We understand her a little better with another decade under our belts, don't we? While it is good to reflect and see just how far you've come, please don't make a habit out of looking back, unless it's to smile over a great memory because you're not going that way. You're moving forward with more resolve than ever before. You are strong, smart, beautiful, and you are gonna own it! You and Jesus, Momma, you and Jesus.

Ahem, excuse me. Hey, Supergirl! Miss Fourty! Yes, ma'am, I am talking to you. Don't get defensive, nobody's trying to take your hard-earned crown. I was just gonna help you straighten it a bit. Listen, you're almost there, the kids are just about out of the house, and you'll finally come home to a quiet space. Ahh! I'm proud of you! You have grown so much in your faith and really developed spiritual maturity. There's so much you want to share with those younger versions of yourself, but the dang hot flashes and brain fog—ugh! You will get through menopause, honey, I promise. It's gonna take a whole lot of Jesus and coffee, but you're gonna be alright. You are! It's not over; it's just getting started.

Hollerin' at my seasoned soul sisters. Yes! My elegant yet bold, my passionate and purpose-driven fifty and fabulous girls who are rich with a treasure trove of experiential wisdom! Yeah, I hear you! I feel you! I know, Sis! After fifty-plus years of experience doing this female thing, one would expect that we'd have it all perfected by now. Girl, just stop that; you know better! Life is a process. Yes, a lot has changed and it doesn't look like what we thought it would. Bags under the eyes, gray hair, muffin top, but hey, a little patina adds value and it isn't ever gonna dull your shine, sister! You know, the glow that comes from inside your soul! That full-faced, non-rehearsed, throw your head back laugh that sounds like bells of Christmas joy. What about that soft, knowing smile-the one where the slight edges of your mouth turn up, the one your daughter, your nieces, and those other younger girls have come to rely on as the assurance signal that they need? Yes, maybe the crow's feet are etched a little deeper, but so is the warmth in those insightful eyes that see with a rich love and understanding that only time and experience can cultivate. All those grooves and crevices, they are the markers of wisdom! They are our military stripes—evidence of courage, conviction, and grit that was meant to harden but instead strengthened and somehow even softened us. Yes, my sisters, we have put in some time. We've prayed our way through births, deaths, marriages, divorces, moves, gains, losses, laughter, trials, and all the other changes that happened both in us and around us. So now, at this *not yet old but certainly no longer young* phase of life, we are equipped, prepared, studied, and we have the grace and favor to show the ones coming behind us how it's done. We no longer have the need to believe we have it all figured out and are more learning-based than ever before, and we are not only willing, but eager to be the hands and feet of God, paying it forward, grateful for all we've come through.

Collectively, **all you girls**, those of every age and stage, **this book is dedicated to you!** It's for you in every way and for every season of the journey called life! So read it, pass it on, and gift it to another. Find a sister and love each other, encourage one another, mentor each other, stand for each other, pray for each other, and *unite*!

Yes, to all the girls of the world, I wrote this book for *you,* straight from my heart, with a prayer that perhaps you could glean a few wisdom nuggets that have been hard-earned and cultivated along my journey. We CAN change our thinking. We CAN make a difference if we learn to slay the *real* enemy and lovingly show the younger ones how to stop drawing their swords on each other, because Sis, it's true ~ we rise by lifting others and we are mighty when united—with Him and with each other!

Arise, sisters!

Love,
Kim

There is an Encourager Inside of You

Hey, Sis,

Please know that you, exactly who you are, where you are, and right in the middle of what you're walking through, can hold another's hand and heart with compassion and kindness. We don't have to have it all-together to love our sisters, to cheer on our tribe, or to lend another's heart some rhythm. Your voice matters and we need each other!

Keep caring and keep initiating, Sis. It's the love we give away that sustains us, promise! Remember, Jesus said, "Love others as I have loved you." With something as simple as a smile, a hello and a simple gesture, you have the power to change the trajectory of another's day and maybe even impact their life! You see, attitudes are contagious and our job is to spread joy around like confetti ~ especially when we don't feel like it. Yes…being kind matters, but being generous with encouragement can be life changing…not just for the recipient, but also the giver. My grandmother used to say that when you are a blessing to others, the heavens open up and God looks after those who love others. We never know where another is walking and how just a simple gesture can profoundly affect them. When you get an *unction* to say hello and smile ~ do it, Sis! It is so easy to get wrapped up in our own thoughts, that we often miss opportunities to BE the blessing. John Maxwell said it best:

> *Everyone has the potential to become an encourager. You don't have to be rich. You don't have to be a genius. You don't have to have it all together. All you have to do is care about people and initiate. (John C. Maxwell)*

Get out of Autopilot

Hey, Sis,

Ever feel like you just need an adventure, a vacation, or a break but you're bound up in fretting and anxiety has such a grip on you that you just can't relax? Let go! Just do it, because living in fear stinks. It stifles us. We get paralysis analysis and do nothing but circle 'round that block again and again. I'm so over it, so over the enemy binding me up like that. Aren't you?

Kids have the right idea. They approach each day with excitement, as if life is one big adventure! Everything is a discovery because they stay curious and open, whereas we grownups are preoccupied with our to-do lists and get so busy formulating judgments about everything and everyone around us, we miss out on a ton of beauty. How many times have you arrived at your destination and thought, *Man, I don't even know how I got here. It's like I was in autopilot mode.*

So often we get caught up in trying to control our environment, thinking we must be surrounded by a certain *type* of people—usually those like us who do things our way and never stretch us outside our comfort zone. Chances are, we miss out on some good learning opportunities and quite possibly some great friendships as a result, all because we strive to be in control. Of what though? Seriously, what outside our own selves do we honestly think we are controlling? "Well, I like order," you say. Hmmm… Could there really be order around you when there is no order in you? Who set that order? Okay, that's another conversation; I digress.

Back to adventure, if you are tired of maintaining, not really living but just existing, drained from the monotony and false sense of safety in the well-worn path, then step out! *Step out* of fear, give up the need to control, because a confident woman of God knows who she is and welcomes expansion. So venture into the unknown; don't be resistant to growing opportunities.

Pray each day:

> *Lord, help me to see others as You do and lead me to those who will help me grow and whom I can bless in return. Show me what is within the safety of expansion without compromising Your standards. Teach me to have the faith of a child, trusting that if I will venture out, You, God, will send angels before me. Give me a heart so full of gratitude and appreciation that fear has no room to grow. I trust You! Amen.*

Go on Girl ~ Get your adventure on!

Love,
Kim

Don't be so busy scrolling other people's adventures that you forget to experience your own.

—KD

Shake It Off

Hey, Sis,

This is for the gal waking up to another Saturday morning of lackluster.

I mean, you got to sleep in. Yay! You have no *plans* though. Moreover, you don't have much energy for the umpteen million projects currently in progress, and the thought of where to start makes you want to go right back between those bed covers, right?

It's okay. You're okay. Promise, this isn't every day of the rest of your life! Look, we all face doldrums now and again; it's the human condition. *Meh* just happens but that doesn't mean you have to go assigning labels to yourself like non-productive, underachiever, procrastinator, boring, dull, without meaning or purpose, or even lazy.

In fact, the only thing looking at everyone else's activities does is tempt you to compare yourself, and that's not good for you, nor is your limited perspective a full picture of their life's entirety. So don't go there, please.

What we see, hear, and *think* have powerful abilities to shape our lives. If we're honest, not everything available for us to visually feast on is good for us.

Life moves in seasons, friend; it's always changing. Guess what else? You do too, and this mood you find yourself in, it's not permanent. So I'll tell you like I tell myself and have taught my grandson, *feel it then shake it off*!

Pray, eat, be thankful for *your* blessings, take a minute to focus inwardly and look up to the God who loves you fiercely, and trust that you're gonna be alright.

Take care of you, feed your spirit, worship your Creator, turn on some music, and dance your way out of the frame of mind that wants to shackle you into envy, sadness, and negative thinking.

You matter!

So shake off those doldrums, and hey, you can always come over to my place. I've got cake, and cake cures a lot!

I'm hugging you right now.

Love,
Kim

Oh, and one more thing: ain't nobody ever stayed miserable while grabbing someone else's heart and giving them much needed encouragement. So go love your people, your neighbors, or even a stranger, even if it's a little uncomfortable. It changes things, mostly us!

*Most folks are as happy as they
make up their minds to be.*

—Abraham Lincoln

Up in Your Feels?

The weed of offense can wreak havoc
on the garden of our hearts.

—KD

Listen, Sis,

We women are passionate creatures! We love deeply and likewise experience profound hurt, but living all up in your feelings 24-7 is not a healthy way to function in life. It leads to regret over abrupt responses, the ones we wish had just paused before we spoke aloud, and can negatively affect every area of our lives.

We have all been the recipient of offense, likewise we've caused another to be offended. It's many times unfair and unwarranted, but it's *always* unproductive!

My grandmother used to tell me that everything in the physical realm has a spiritual counterpart in the unseen realm. Meaning this: if you choose to harbor the spirit of offense, you are setting yourself up for its divisive and destructive counterparts which are pride, indignation, fear, and gossip to take residence as well. The end result is unforgiveness and crippled love. Without love, Godly love, we cannot grow, produce good fruit, or mature in our walk.

Forgiveness is the key. Even if you don't *feel* like forgiving, make the *choice* to forgive. Simply state out loud in prayer that you release your anger and hurt and that with God's help you choose to forgive the one who offended you. Your feelings don't change instantly, but by your own confession and declaration you are giving God room to let His Spirit work within you, and your feelings will catch up. Just as we cannot be tossed to and fro by everything that happens in our broken society, we cannot allow bitterness to take root over an offense. Look, hear me clearly, I am not suggesting that every person who has offended you is of darkness—reread that again if you need to and please don't misunderstand me. Legitimate, unfair situations and circumstances cause hurt. People are human and we women are fiercely protective of our loved ones. The act of being offended over a wrongdoing is not evil, it is a natural human response. What I am talking about here is the holding onto of bitterness and unforgiveness or misappropriated anger that will give the enemy a foothold into our minds and hearts. Remember your armor! Our feelings are natural and a justified initial response. It is when left unchecked and allowed to fester that they can lead us to very dry, bitter places.

We need to practice the art of changing what we can and accepting what we cannot, and we do this through prayer and meditation, asking God to guide us into healthy and proportionate responses. Our feelings are not bad or wrong, but we must keep them in check. Either we rule them or they rule us! (Took me a while to embrace that truth!) Don't live up in your feels, girlfriend! Instead, root yourself in the truth that *God is good* and *trustworthy*! We can release our disappointments to Him and let Him do what only He can so we are able to walk in love.

Tend to your garden Sis,
Kim

She-motional?

Hey, Sis,

Being she-motional isn't a bad thing.

Look, God gave us feelings to serve as indicators of where we are mentally and those feelings are purposeful, but they are not the directors of our life and often don't serve as the basis for healthy decision-making.

So then, what does?

If it glorifies God, honors His precepts, and passes the litmus test of the following scripture, then it is a yes for us! That thing we call the conscious, it is the very Spirit of God leading and prompting us. There are two screenings I like to filter my ideas through before they become actions. This isn't just a suggestion for what our minds should think on, but also a gauge to help us make choices that when we look back on our activities, we will have peace about them.

Celebrate being female. Christ did. The first person he showed himself to after the resurrection was a woman! Celebrate all the female feels. It's our tribe talk; it's the stuff our sisters all understand too! The mind is powerful and we must learn to govern it in order to be intentional about our iving. I don't

want to be blown like a leaf in the wind ~ been there
~ done that ~ not our highest and best form of living!
If you want to take authority over how you live you
must begin with changing your thinking patterns

You can do this,
Kim

*Whatever is true, whatever is noble,
whatever is right, whatever is pure,
whatever is lovely, whatever is
admirable—if anything is excellent
or praiseworthy, think about such
things. (Philippians 4:8)*

Consider the Fields

Hey, Sister friend,

I know you're confused. It doesn't make sense how things played out. This isn't the outcome you were anticipating, so I can see how grave disappointment might set in. Don't let it. Remember that life moves in seasons.

We know nature operates in seasons: winter, spring, summer, and fall. But the seasons of life are a difficult concept for us because that requires change and we like permanency. In fact, sometimes we confuse time with quality, erroneously believing if it isn't long term then it isn't legitimate. There is only one thing meant for eternity—our relationship with God.

Consider the fields.

Sometimes we work in a field, tilling the soil, planting the seeds, caring for the crops, but then when it's harvest time, we don't get to take part in the reaping. Other times we haven't lifted a finger to contribute to the farming process, yet we are gifted with a bountiful harvest that we never broke a sweat for and are still invited to dine at the farmer's table.

Sometimes we plant, sometimes we sow, and sometimes we harvest—it's all about seasons. There is a time for all things and a purpose to every season under heaven. Trust that in due time you will be provided for and keep on being a blessing to others.

"Let us not lose heart in doing good for in due time we will reap" (Galatians 6:9).

Things aren't always going to go as planned—that's a certainty! When all your efforts fail to produce the desired outcome, when the job doesn't become your career, when the relationship ends seemingly premature, when your heartfelt gesture isn't received well, and when they fail to appreciate you, hear you, respect you, honor you, or even respond to you, know that God is working in all seasons and He has a plan.

Detach from expectations and trust that He is working all things for our good in every season.

Sis, spring always follows winter. Remember that *you will* bloom again!

Love,
Kim

[She] is like a tree planted by streams of water that yields [her] fruit in season, and [her] leaf doesn't wither and all she does will prosper. (Psalm 1:3)

Just Not Meant for You

Hey, Sis,

Not everyone is for you.

Now hang on, before you let your mind go into defense mode thinking *If they aren't for me, then they must be against me.* That's not the thought path we are traveling today.

Perhaps a more concise way of expressing this truth would be to say that not everyone is **meant** for you—not meant to stay, not meant to have a long-term role, not meant for an extended, ongoing relationship in your life. No matter how fun or friendly, not everyone is good for you, either!

We've all heard the saying "Season, reason, and lifetime," right? People come into our lives for a reason. The rub exists when we try to push an encounter into something more than just that. When we ignore signs that tell us something is off about a relationship, we run the risk of exposing ourselves to influences that can negatively alter our thinking and take us off the path to our destiny.

Good judgment, sound reasoning, and human logic will often caution us toward or away from what or who isn't meant for us, but these mechanisms can fail us too. We vacillate between an attempt to be compassionate and not wanting to offend anyone to even convincing ourselves that we must be *open* to growth, telling ourselves that there must be something we can glean from this person. What doesn't fail us is called discernment. It's beyond intuition because it's a spiritual knowing from God.

Look, I cannot tell you the number of times when I was initially resistant to a person or situation that in the end, turned out to be a fantastic learning experience ~ so hear me when I say that YES~we can learn from all experiences. But the caveat remains ~ we must not latch onto anyone out of loneliness. Or boredom. Or clutch people so hard they cannot pass through. Those meant to walk alongside us do not require coaxing, begging or pleading. Make room for their exit.

Simply put, we must be studious about whom we allow to speak into our lives, especially when it comes to teaching us about our faith walk and spiritual things. Your closest companions have a very powerful role in your life…choose wisely…be selective. Culture tells us we need to have large followings and be popular…covenant assures us that God directs our paths and provides all we need, including bringing the right ones at the right time! If someone tells you they have a *word from the Lord*, check it against scripture. God's messages will never contradict His word! Never ever! If we ask Him for wisdom, He will grant us opportunities to develop it. He will instill a cautionary wisdom in us, making us prudent in discretion.

So while there are well-meaning Christians who will boldly minister to you from a place of sincerity, I encourage you to be just as bold when you take each person, situation, and thought before God in prayer. God is not the author of confusion or chaos. So don't let those who aren't meant for you push their agenda without seeking discernment. We can lovingly step away.

We are called to love and can do so from a healthy distance, when necessary. Not everyone is for you, sister friend, and that's okay. *He* is for you.

Of all the gifts we can receive, discernment and wisdom are those that will propel us into that which IS meant for us! May it be said of us that we chose covenant over culture!

Love,
Kim

More than Invited!

Hey, Sis,

The luncheon, the girl's weekend, the shopping spree—so many invitations out there that it's hard to say yes to all of them. Then there are the invites you don't receive, the ones that have the ability to wreak as much havoc on your heart as the stress of juggling your schedule around does for those that you did receive.

No one wants to feel left out. None of us likes being made to feel unwelcome. Doesn't matter that we can't always attend, we want the option to, right? I know. It hurts ~ I've been there.

Here's the thing we must remember. Although we were made for community, not every invitation is a healthy activity for us and we cannot hear from God (or sort out our own thoughts) if we are constantly running around with chaotically full social calendars. Downtime has become taboo in our modern culture, yet it is precisely what we require to *be still*. Our culture doesn't promote being still and we worker bees, overachieving types think that busy equals productive. It doesn't. Those are two very different things.

If we could shift our thinking to embrace the truth that we were already invited to the only event that truly matters for eternity, being chosen by Christ, it would take the sting and confusion out of all other events, whether we're included or not.

Simply stated, it all ties back to identity. We are more than the selected, we are the *chosen*! Can we finally let go of fretting over who is doing what and why we weren't a part of it? That's not what confirms our value. If we are honest, we have all left someone out somewhere along the line. Sometimes God is protecting us from that which isn't meant for us, so let's reserve our *best* yes for Him! Run to that which feeds your spirit over simply being a yes girl and staying "busy".

You are more than invited, more than welcome—you are chosen!

Have you RSVP'd heaven's invite? Hope so. I wanna see ya there, and I'll save you a seat at my table, girlfriend!

Love,
Kim

Grace When Wounded

Hey, Sis,

You're hurt. I see the look of disappointment in your face. You're caught somewhere between mad and sad, and that's okay. Feel your feelings, then pray, forgive, and let it go, please. If you hold onto it, it's going to get into your spirit. Hurt feelings must be worked through and not allowed to sit and fester. Otherwise, we end up with a *wounded spirit*, and that's not what we are called to.

Your spirit is the key to your future and above all else, Proverbs 4:23 says we should guard it with *all diligence* (the Bible translates the word for *heart* and *spirit* interchangeably).

Pride, bitterness, a wounded spirit, and unforgiveness are the kinds of things that weaken us and leave us open and vulnerable to junk, while closing us off to the good stuff God has in store for us. So lay it down before you get all puffed up over it. Give that pain to Jesus, and he'll replace it with peace.

Listen, I hear you, it was rotten and unfair, and you didn't deserve it. Still, give her/him the same grace you've been given, because your spirit is your responsibility—not hers, not his, not theirs. It's between you and God, so look to Jesus, forgive, and stay humble and open. Keep growing, keep learning, and keep loving. You're worth it! I'm rooting for you!

Much love,
Kim

The weed of offense can wreak havoc on the garden of our hearts—choking out the very life from all that was meant to bloom inside you! Let it go. Choose peace.

K.D.

Still Isn't Small ...

Hey, Sis,

We can be still without being small.

It's true. Turning up the volume doesn't guarantee we are being heard. In fact the softer you speak, the more folks must be intentional about listening. Test this one. Try it out and you'll see that when we speak just above a whisper, people lean in to hear us. It piques their curiosity and defies the saying, *The wheel that squeaks the loudest gets oiled.*

When the whole wide world is vying for attention, trying to be big, bold, and out-front, you, my dear sister, can command the listener with non-action even more than when you take dramatic measures.

"But if I am too quiet, won't I be overlooked? If I don't speak with authority, will I be taken seriously? I'm competing with so many to be heard and seen." Nah... *Stinkin' thinkin' right there. You compete with no one! Say it out loud...*

I COMPETE WITH NOONE!

Remember, meek isn't weak! We are strong when we are leaning into truth, allowing our words to be saturated with love and we *can* do all things through

Christ. We are keeping our affections directed toward the one who sustains us—Jesus!

We can pull back without shrinking when our value is rooted in who God says we are, rather than based on the attention, approval, validation, and acceptance of others.

There is only one you and the world needs you to be authentic ~ not comparing or competing, but simply BEING!!

You're amazing, Girl!

Love,
Kim

Don't You Do It!

Hey, Sis,

Don't you do it! Well, not anymore, okay?

It is so tempting (and easy) to get stuck in that trap of thinking the number of likes on a social media post equals our worth. So many of us do it. We depend on Instagram comments and Facebook likes, believing they are the measurement of how cared for, respected, heard, seen, and loved we are. It's like a high school popularity marker. What a distorted measure for likability or value we have succumbed to.

Look, I get it, we all want to matter. We all need validation. None of us want to feel insignificant. The thing is, *we are so much more valuable than this*!

God sees us, all of us—our deepest most secret parts! He sees way down into the secret garden of our hearts and only He can assign our value. We are priceless to Him. So trust me when I tell you, numbers lie! What the bathroom scale says, what the insights on your social media page reflect, how many friends you have on Facebook, and even the number in your bank account—*none* of these define your value!

So post, tweet, snap away, sis, but do so because it needs to be said versus looking for a reaction. Just because they don't comment doesn't mean they didn't see it or that it didn't impact them. Just because we don't see the butterfly effect doesn't mean it isn't happening.

We will never stop the spirals, never change our thinking, until we unlearn and stand up to the so-called social norms that try to box us into some false sense of validation. You're already enough!

God's eyes are on you. His ears are attentive and He is leaning down to whisper, "I see you, my daughter, and I love you right where you are, just as you are, and you are sealed by Me."

You are defined by your Maker, and He has assigned your value as follows:

> *She is more precious than rubies;*
> *nothing you can desire is more pre-*
> *cious than her. (Proverbs 3:15)*

This particular arena of being liked has been a huge struggle for me. As a young girl I had an insatiable need to have validation. Was it daddy issues, a broken home, estrangement from an absent parent – who knows…maybe all of the above. While it is important to seek for understanding on the big "why" behind our so-called issues – I am certain that what takes even more of a precedence of the knowing why is the chutzpah to change our thinking and recognize that we must love ourselves properly before we are able to love others. How do we do that? We remember WHOSE we are! Stand boldly and confidently in the truth of our unique beauty and remember that we have purpose inside of us…destiny does not require approval!

I am praying that you look in the mirror today and God gives you fresh eyes to see yourself as the amazing creature you are!

With so much love,
Kim

Lean into the Light-Maker

Don't give rejection the authority
to assassinate your identity, sis!
Remember—rejection is often protection.

—KD

Hey, Sis,

It's easy to get discouraged when, despite our best efforts, things don't go as planned. I understand that disappointment. I truly do. We get weary, don't we?

Sometimes, even our most honorable intentions are going to be misunderstood and things go awry. You keep being a do-gooder anyway! God's got you and knows where your heart is. Just because you don't get to see or be a part of the end result, know that your role matters!

Let go of the outcome, release any expectation other than the satisfaction of a job well done, and continue giving, helping, caring, and extending kindness.

We will be happier creatures when we realize that we aren't in control of anything but our own actions. Stages, phases, seasons, and always a reason—always!

(Even if we don't understand.) So keep doing your part and let go so the next phase can commence.

Your kindness matters!

A friend once told me something that made such sense.

God calls us to be *like* Jesus, not to try to *be a GOD* for others—let Him work *in* and *through* you, sis. It's not your job to fix everything and everyone, so stop being attached to the outcome and remember *you* aren't the light-maker—you're just a beautiful reflection of it!

I needed to hear that. I suspect you do too. Don't grow weary, friend! I'm rooting for you, but Jesus, He is *championing* for you! Lean into the Light-Maker. You were made to shine!

Love,
Kim

Let Your Heart Beat Again

You've got to serve your way out of sorrow, girl!

—KD

To my broken-hearted Sister,

When we get to the last leg of grief, pushing past all the many ways it feels so unfair, the financial burden it caused, the loneliness that resulted, the many abrupt changes that followed, at the end of loss's journey, it's the finality of death that engulfs us.

Experts have identified *five stages of grief* as an unordered combination of the following: denial, anger, bargaining, depression, and acceptance.

Seems like a rather tidy way to classify and categorize our feelings, doesn't it? As if simply labeling the gamut of emotions we experience will bring order to the mourning process.

Yes, the finality grips us. The conversation we didn't know would be the last, the holidays we will have to endure without them, the permanent absence of their presence in our day-to-day lives—it can all be unbearable unless we know the truth.

We are given a lifespan to live as human beings, but we are spiritual beings having a human experience—not the other way around. The spirit doesn't die, it doesn't end her. The *heart* goes on, sis! As believers, we will be reunited with our loved ones one day. We *will* see them again in a place where no pain exists. People die, hope does not. Oh it hides, it seems lost forever, but hope has a name—Jesus! Lean into Him, take all that pain and anguish to Him; He understands. He has tasted death, even going into hell to take back the power death had over creation.

Those five stages are defined to help us more clearly understand our emotions so we can make concerted efforts to process grief. Healing, true healing, comes through the person of Jesus, by His Holy Spirit working in us.

Submit that sorrow to God, sis, because holding onto your pain like a badge of honor will only prevent you from living out your God-given purpose. God knew and it didn't surprise Him. He still has a plan for you; embrace it.

Allow the Father to collect those shattered pieces and create a beautiful mosaic of healing and restoration. *Come into agreement* and tell your proverbial heart that it is truly okay to beat again, sis.

With so much love,
Kim

Humble Pie

Hey, Sis,

We've all tasted it—humble pie. It's about as appetizing as last year's fruitcake, right?

Look at the ingredients:

one-part big mouth
three parts bad discretion
a teaspoon of arrogance
a pinch of pride

Mix them all together, and you've got a recipe for near disaster!

The interesting thing about the word *humble* is that it's often confused with *weakness*. Humility, by definition, is freedom from pride or arrogance. Being humble is a sign of quiet strength and should never be confused with lacking self-confidence or being less than strong! The question is, where does your confidence come from? Is it rooted in the knowledge that you are a child of the Most High God, unique and purposefully created to be THE ONLY YOU THERE IS or have you fallen prey to the faulty thinking that would influence us to believe that something as fleeting as your financial station, your title at work, or your outward appearance is where your confidence comes from? If you pay attention, you'll find that most of the time, when someone is haughty with or toward us, demonstrating arrogance or being prideful, it is actually rooted in deep insecurity–they say things they later regret and pride keeps them from being humble enough to own and correct it. A lot of hurt feelings and damage to our relationships could be avoided if we learn to govern our tongues and keep our opinions to ourselves ~ because honestly, our feelings, thoughts and opinions are subject to change, but the words once spoken cannot be unheard. Godly confidence is a beautiful thing ~ pride and arrogance, not so much!

Momma used to tell me, "You don't have to say everything you think." I learned that keeping my mouth shut was a surefire way to avoid eating humble pie. It doesn't taste good. It kind of makes your breath stink, y'all.

Practicing the pause is a brilliant way to avoid a nasty ole' side dish of humble pie!

Hush until you heal,
Kim

Identity Crisis

Hey, Sis, who are you?

Our parents name us. We receive nicknames throughout our lives, names by which we are referred. People can identify us by our title, our name, our SSN, and even recognize us by our outward appearance, but please hear me when I tell you only *the one* who gave you your very life, created you, and only your manufacturer has the right *and the authority* to give you your identity!

Circumstances may have made things difficult for you, but they aren't powerful enough to define you. Your history may have marked you, but it is not authorized to label you. Those derogatory names you were called, those things that unfairly victimized and pained you deeply that require years of purposeful and intentional work to get beyond—none of them have the power to shape the totality of who it is you have been created to be!

Yes, all of those can influence you, impact you, affect you, and even damage you to a degree, but they cannot negate or alter *who God says you are*! You are not defined by your behavior, your feelings, or your situation. No ideology or vain philosophy of our culture can determine your true identity! Your creator and Father God Almighty has defined you as chosen and beloved, born of a royal race for priesthood in Christ Jesus! Every single aspect of your person, including the individual components of your physicality, hair texture, size, shape, skin color, talents, and personality is by design and *on purpose*. There are *no* accidents, no happenstance. Although we get surprised by life and the unplanned (by us), we are assured by His word that we are made in the image of *God*! We are each a unique expression of His image with a primary purpose of worshiping and communing in intimate relationship with Him so that we can also be in a healthy and rewarding relationship with others as we reflect His light, pointing others to His glory.

That is who you are—you simply have to know it, believe it, and walk in it! Our faith in His Son, Jesus, provides us the mercy required to walk forward in our humanity and receive the grace that equips us to do all He has designed us to do, my sisters! Purpose and promise and destiny are not just rah-rah, feel-good terminology. No, they are what we were made to experience as daughters of the Creator!

Where we get tripped up is in the functionality of life. We eagerly attempt to rush headlong into our fleshy plans and desires, and quickly learn it is only when we have the indwelling of the Holy Spirit, when we surrender to being temples, that we are empowered to live out the calling and fulfill the great commission of our innate and intentional design. So what does that look like? What habits serve your relationship with God? What intentional practices are you engaging in that position you for hearing and being led by the Lord? Do you daily surrender through obedience?

> *Who sits on the throne of your heart, because there is only room for one! (Matthew 6:24)*

Words Can Be Weapons

Hey, Sis, use your words wisely.

We hear a phrase like "weapons of mass destruction" and immediately associate it with war. That's not incorrect thinking. In fact, it is precisely what is happening all around us every single day. Countries, cities, and villages are always at war. We in the US haven't seen full-blown war since the days of WWII, but trust me when I tell you that there is warfare happening all around us and even within us—spiritual warfare, that is.

Ironically, of all the weapons we forge, the most powerful and destructive is often our words. We speak out of anger, fear, hurt, pain, brokenness, bitterness, and usually a very limited perspective. Those words sit inside the heart and mind of others indefinitely wreaking havoc, eroding away at the very core of another like masterful weaponry does a city.

Like fiery arrows projecting from the quiver of our mouths, weaponized words infiltrate our minds and pierce our hearts. That isn't the end though because they ruminate, playing on repeat and causing further wounding until eventually they arc out of the recipient's heart to go forth hurting yet another. This is mass destruction at its finest, perpetuating over and over.

What if we took authority over our words? What if we chose to believe we could offer healing balm through our speech? What if we chose to speak life instead of weaponizing another with our words? I challenge you today to envision that your words are like an injection into the soul of another. Will you inoculate them or infect them?

Now hear me good on this one. *I do not* have this mastered—not by a long shot! However, I am intentional and mindfully improving every day and you can too! Ask the Holy Spirit to put a guard over your mouth because, sis, your power is sometimes in your silence. Let that sink in, okay? Marinate on it. Your dignity, your self-respect, and your ability to walk with poise and purpose hinge on your ability to tame that tongue.

Fix Us Fixers

Hey, Sis,

As women we are hardwired to want to fix things, resolve issues, correct problems, and prevent turmoil. It's innate, born from an honest place of desiring peace for our loved ones and wanting to offer the value of our experience to help rectify any wrongs and prevent potential misgivings. It's a beautiful thing, really. When God fashioned us, he called us helpmates. We possess the divine gifts of serving in the roles of counselors, caretakers, coaches, and encouragers to all those whose lives we touch. If not careful and mindful of our limitations however, we can develop a need to control that and it will taint every noble effort we make. It starts with laying down that prideful inclination to be needed and surrendering it to become purposeful instead. Remember, we are to be vessels not vehicles.

God calls us to be like Jesus, not try to be *God* to others. Allowing Him to work in and through us is key. It's not our job to fix everything and everyone.

Do what you are called and impressed to do with no expectations then stand upright and release all potential outcomes, sis. Let go and let God! For real, open the tightly clenched fists of your heart and release what you aren't meant to carry. He is not only able but oh so willing to move in that circumstance. Make room for Him to work.

May we come to understand that we are meant to play a part in each other's lives, not a role, always pointing to the only One who can fix it. Those you love and so desperately want to help, they need Him more than they need you. Our job is to love them. Love, the simplest and hardest thing of all.

Fix us, God, in all your great mercy. Fix us fixers, please! It's my prayer for all our zealous hearts. We can entrust them to Him.

A Note about the Ebb and Flow of Friendship

To my ever-so-much-more over-the-top kinda Sis,

Ever been accused of being extreme? Needing balance? Being too much of something or not enough of another? Have people pulled away from you because of your intensity level? Or even been told you are just a little too salty for their taste?

When someone works late every night, goes in on weekends and is consumed with their own career, we applaud their efforts and lament on them having a stellar work ethic. We admire the parent who is consumed with their child or children, running themselves ragged driving to and from the practice field, dance studio, or extracurricular events, over-booked and hyper committed, leaving little to no time for themselves or others. We respectfully label them as devoted and family oriented. When an activist is persistent to generate change or heighten awareness to the point they participate in demonstrations, lobby the offices of elected officials, hold meetings, and host marches, we celebrate them as passionate world changers. When a Christian becomes devoted and sold out for their God-given purpose we call them a *Jesus freak*, a fundamentalist, an over-the-top religious fanatic, or even Christian crazy, accusing them of being antiquated, unrealistic, and occasionally declaring they *don't live in the real world.* I know this because I have been both the accused and the accuser, and I have learned that by nature, people want to be around people who make them feel most comfortable. As long as you are being encouraging and supportive, you're called a friend, but as soon as you challenge, confront, or correct someone with the truth, they pull away. You have become *too* something for them or *not enough* of what they need and expect.

We all want to be accepted and gain the approval of our contemporaries, our friends, our peers, or others. Claiming that no one should be made to feel like an outcast, or like they don't belong or fit in. For me, it comes down to whom you are looking to be accepted by. Whose approval do you seek?

The closer I've drawn into my relationship with God, the more lifestyle changes I've made. Not because a religious faction or sector has commanded my compliance, but because in my pursuit of His will being accomplished in my life, my heart and understanding opened, prompting a shift in my desires.

This resulted in steep changes in many of my relationships, but not with her and for that I value her and her friendship immensely! She doesn't necessarily espouse the same creed I do. We aren't always on the exact same page. Sometimes we differ on issues, but our opinions never lead to dissension, rejection, or abandonment. Instead, they challenge us to examine our convictions and create a richer attachment to them because we respect one another instead of trying to change one another, fully recognizing that it would be the Holy Spirit's job versus ours. We are sincerely interested in what the other has to say and truly want what we as individuals believe is best for ourselves to be given room to manifest in the other.

We are learning-based and open to each other's ideas. Because she stretches me and challenges me to be more, I hold her friendship in the highest of regard. She isn't a *yes* girl, she will tell me no if she doesn't agree. No staunchness exists between us.

If we are in different places, we seek to understand the other's position, never allowing it to compromise our own. Our differences do not make us uncomfortable, they make us unique. There is a unity between us as friends that doesn't exist among many, even more so than I've seen present among folks with the same religious views. She and I aren't the same denomination, we aren't in the same socioeconomic demographic. We didn't go to the same high school (okay, that's only funny if you're from St. Louis), but we both share a reverence for God as Sovereign. We both aspire to become who He wants us to be as people. We both, although possessing strong leadership traits, have servant hearts and that comes only from God. She has been appointed into my life because she pushes, stretches, and causes me to grow!

There is an ebb and flow to friendships and that's okay. We need all kinds of grace to maintain healthy relationships and not everyone has to be *like us* to be of great value in our lives. Where some of my relationships have regressed because of my spiritual progression, this one has remained firm and perhaps even been enriched. She and I recognize there will always be those who say we're too much of one thing and not enough of another, but we aren't swayed by people's opinions or demands of us. Our identity is who we are to God. We accept and own *Whose* we are above the perception of *who* people say we are, and that gives us the freedom to love ourselves and each other.

While I may be too much or not enough for some, I remain grateful for her God-given friendship and the security I have found in belonging to God (through Jesus) first! May each of us have at least one of *her* in our lives.

Thank you, friend.

My grandmother used to say that if you treat a person as if they are already who you know they can be, they have a much better chance of reaching their full God-given potential. (KD)

Quit the Quick Fix

Hey, Sis,

Everything is instant and microwaveable, so just add water and stir—yuck! Don't you ever hanker for a good ole pot of slow-cooked soup or smoked brisket? Seriously, it takes the barista at Starbucks longer to prepare a cup of coffee than most of our lunches take to eat.

Slow it all down, turn down the noise, pull back some, and find a place to recoup and recenter—a place to heal. A little separation can help you regain your bearings, secure your footing, and prep you to make forward motion again, instead of this going-in-circles pattern that leaves you dizzy and feeling displaced from your very self.

Are you sucked into the quick fix mentality? So desperate to understand how you got here, in this place of utter discombobulation, that you attempt to trace it back, looking for signs and some measurable evidence of a culprit. Finding the exhaustion leaves you just this side of giving a damn about the route as much as you long for the road out. Ever been there?

A friend once told me, "If it was five miles in, it would be five miles out." So stop with the need for instant fixes. Take time, make time, and spend time on *you*—mentally, physically, and spiritually. Give the dough time for the yeast to do its job, then *rise*!

Don't rush the process, for it is there that we do our best growing.

Take your time,
Kim

We Are Instruments, Not Tools!

Hey, Sis,

When loving somebody hinders our ability to tend to our own lives well, it's not love, it's codependency. We are uncomfortable watching them struggle, but sometimes we need to let a person go through their self-created hard time so they can learn and grow. Protecting them from the consequences of their choices will hinder their maturity and steal our peace.

None of us want to see another suffer because we are full of compassion, but we are not created to rescue others—that's God's job. We are called to pray for them, guide them by our example, and show them that there is a better way to live. Trust me, sis, there are plenty of folks who truly need and will appreciate our assistance, those whom it will help versus enable. There is a difference.

Our desire isn't to see anyone struggle, especially those we love—it hurts our hearts. Our longing for comfort isn't a bad thing, but when we try to be *pain blockers*, we actually cheat them because *pain has a purpose.*

It is in the pain and discomfort where responsibility, discipline, obedience, self-governing, and maturity are developed. There is a threshold that must be reached so pain and discomfort can prompt them to make changes. The most loving thing you can do for another is stop letting them lean on you to the point of hindering their ability to develop the skills to be able to depend on themselves. Maybe if we stop playing God, they'll stop blaming Him.

You may be thinking, *What about grace, mercy, and love?* Hear my heart when I tell you that sometimes, administering grace means getting out of the way, that dispensing mercy means letting them face their own mistakes, and that love, healthy love, means detaching so you can live well and so suffering can do its job for all. There are immeasurable gifts that come with discomfort. Desperation breeds creativity and having unmet needs will prompt us to become reliant on *the source*, not the convenience of other's resources.

From one caring heart to another, please remember that our value and our worth are *not* contingent upon our ability to *fix* anyone. God longs to make us instrumental in the lives of those to whom He leads us, not those who would make us tools for their own personal comfort.

In the name of love, be careful you aren't cheating another out of the gifts of discomfort or the purpose in their pain; even Jesus suffered. I have to remind myself that I don't love my son more than God loved His.

> *So even though Jesus was God's Son, he learned obedience from*

the things he suffered. In this way, God qualified him as a perfect high priest, and he became the source of eternal salvation for all those who obey him. (Hebrews 5:8–9)

The Joy of Surrender

Girlfriend,

Sometimes the mind and the heart just don't agree. It's frustrating when what we know and what we feel are at odds. So as believers, we choose to implement wisdom and discipline, trusting that God will honor our obedience.

Sometimes stuff still goes bad; we don't get the results we hoped for. We can become quietly bitter and a little jaded as a result (maybe you don't experience this, but I sure have). I asked God about this. I told Him I didn't understand it and didn't want to be like that. I asked him to change my heart and show me how to have better responses.

You know what He said? "When you see the act of obedience to Me as the victory, without being attached to the outcome or the results, that's when you'll have joy, my daughter." It got me! Like, I felt it in my belly; I understood. It is our heart's motivation He is after. Sure, He may be pleased with our Christlike behaviors, but our Father *delights* in the submission of our hearts. Our will must bow.

I think that verse about *in spirit and truth* just took on a whole new meaning for me. We can modify our behaviors, but only by His Spirit are we truly transformed.

God, thank you for our salvation in Jesus. Give us pure hearts, O God, and by Your Spirit, as we lay down our will, change our desires and renew our minds!

May your spirit woman rise high above your mind, will, and emotions.

Big love,
Kim

We are called to *meet* people, y'all, not "mete" them. Right where they are from exactly where we are—all of us swimming in *amazing grace*. (KD)

More than Rhetoric

Okay, Sis, I am being raw with you. When you hear me say (or see me post) *"Faith your fears,"* trust me when I say it's more than apropos Bible rhetoric that I'm spouting off with to sound all Christianese-ish. ☺

Girl, I have tried seven ways to Sunday to manage, control, circumvent, prevent, stop, contain, or undo my responses (and even the behavior, words, feelings, and thoughts of others) when fear creeps in to lie to me, and *none*—not one of them—work! Oh, maybe for a short time they dull or anesthetize the situation, but faith in the word of God is the only real solution, the only one with lasting effects. You know why? Because it's true, and the feel-good mechanisms of this world can't do what the truth does.

When the enemy comes at you trying to kill, steal, or destroy, he'll whisper lies into your mind or use the words of another to try to defeat you, and that bald-faced liar has centuries of practice knowing just how to get under your skin too! He is no match for the truth of Jesus though!

I get mad. I get insulted. I allow myself to fall into pity, become full of doubt, think I don't measure up, and if I dwell on some of the things others have said or done to me, I can get depressed, salty, and all the other yuck feels! I know how to argue, fight dirty, and give it as good as anyone, trust me, but that method doesn't work either.

In fact, it causes the dissension to escalate and, in the end, I have bit the apple, drank the poison, and now there are two hurting and angry parties who will typically vomit that garbage onto someone else, recruiting others to sign the petition of hate-mongering. Our flesh wants to be impulsive, but that's not the way of love, and it doesn't leave room for the spirit of God to lead.

I remember calling my grandmother, wanting her to get behind me, and get mad at whomever *did me wrong,* and without fail she would listen and then reply with some version of, "Well, sister, the Lord sees this situation, and He will lead you if you allow Him to, so just pray." This was not at all what I was looking for! I wanted her to get upset along with me, tell me so-n-so was a jerk, pray for their demise, or at least for God to punish them. She didn't. She always spoke the *word* of God because the truth was how she fought battles!

I get tickled looking back because now I hear myself doing the same thing (okay, not every single time, but more often than not and quicker than I used to). If there were a shortcut, I would have found it by now because I'm kind of relentless (occasionally stubborn too).

What I am trying to tell you is that you don't have to get all tied up in knots. You don't have to go off in a corner and cry tears of hopelessness. You don't have to carry around doubt, fear, anxiety, and all the other heavy lies the enemy wants you to believe because you can shut that down with the truth! Even if you feel the effects of the false accusations, or perhaps I should say *especially* when you feel the effects, speak that truth, sis!

On the next page, you'll find the full list of *truths* that combats these lies from the pits of hell! Speak 'em, girl! Declare them out loud! Raise your sword and fight right! We are never going to beat darkness with darkness! We can't defeat hate with hate!

A final note: What prompted this love note is that, just recently, someone tried to tell me who I am and am not, and I caught myself coming into agreement with the lies being spoken at me. Yes, even after seven years of growth, I darn near succumbed to it and called a bestie to help me *walk it out* (and to whine—there, I said it). My sweet *Touchstone* reminded me to remember who(se) I am and to adjust my crown, still my heart, and act like a daughter of the Highest.

Maybe, by sharing it with you, you'll be inclined to do the same.

Imperfect, but perfectly loved,
Kim <3

There is a biblical *truth* for every single lie and I speak my way right back into the promises that I am loved, chosen, and forgiven no matter what the deceiver says!

I began to speak the truth and my countenance shifted because darkness cannot defeat the light! Take that, devil!

My accuser said I am a liability, the truth says I am holy and I share in God's heavenly calling. (Hebrews 3:1)

My accuser said I am a fool, the truth says I have access to God's wisdom. (James 1:5)

My accuser said I am shallow and wishy-washy, the truth says I am firmly rooted and built up in Christ. (Col 2:7)

My accuser said I am a wannabe fraud, the truth says I have been established, anointed, and sealed by God. (2 Cor. 1:21–22)

Look them up, those scriptures. They are our sword and when we speak them, we slay!

Burnt Toast and Spilled Milk

A final letter for you, Sweet Sis,

Even the most basic stuff will go sideways sometimes. It's frustrating, but this is life and perfection is *not* required. You can and most likely will burn the toast and spill the milk! Seriously, how do you burn toast? The toaster's fine, the settings are correct, still it's black, ruined, and smoking.

That is life! Sometimes you can have the best cookware, the fanciest of gadgets, and the perfect recipe, and you still burn the dish. Heck, sometimes you melt the pan—it happens!

Reading this book won't make you any better in the kitchen or at the table of life. It was never intended to bring healing properties, only to direct you to the One who can heal. God uses us to be His voice, His hands, and His feet to minister into the lives of others—even if it is only to help us feel understood. In those times when we feel isolated and unreachable, like no one, not even God himself, could make a difference in our hearts, that's when the best dishes come along. My prayer is that you will be open to conversation about love, friendship, and support, that you will seek out truth in those arenas.

I hope that you will come to a place where you are open to receive.

I pray that you will never give up, that you will never give in.

Press on, my sisters.

Love,
Kim

*There is a lioness within every one of God's daugh-
ters and it is time that she awakens. (Lisa Bevere)*

What finally changed me was loving Jesus more than I disliked myself. ~ KD

About the Author

Kimberly DeAnn is a disciple for Christ on a mission to spread His unconditional, relentless love to others. A servant-leader, mother of five, and Nonnie to her five grandchildren, she endeavors to make a multigenerational impact by helping all women become confident in their God-given identity—to live fearlessly no matter what their age and to step boldly into their unique purpose. Through her multiplatform ministry work as a podcast host, public speaker, study group leader, and writer, she shares *glory stories* to encourage women of all faith backgrounds to embrace grace through the grit of life. "Imperfect but perfectly loved" is the creed that keeps her resolved.